Matchstick Mini is very cl

By Edel Malone

Original concept created, illustrated, and written by Edel Malone. I'm sure you will love these books as much as I do. I know you will enjoy making lasting memories with your child moving forward in all stages of their lives by encouraging your child to tell you what's on their mind throughout their lifetime. Asking questions is the way forward. Check out some of the other Matchstick Mini books. Sizes and colors may vary for printed books.

The Matchstick Mini books are designed to encourage your child to open up and talk about what is on their mind from an early age. The topics covered are related to young children to encourage good communication techniques carrying on into each stage of their lives, keeping safety and values in mind.

OTHER BOOKS FROM MATCHSTICK MINI

Matchstick Mini and safety

Matchstick Mini and others

Matchstick Mini has fun

Matchstick Mini and school

Matchstick is very good

Matchstick Mini is healthy

Matchstick Mini loves looking out of the window, he likes to watch people going by. Matchstick Mini won't climb on the window, he knows it is not safe, Matchstick Mini is very clever.

Matchstick Mini is very clever, he will not go into public toilets on his own without an adult with him. When Matchstick Mini uses the toilet, he always flushes the toilet after he uses it. Matchstick Mini thinks the toilet is magic because when he flushes the toilet the dirty water disappears.

Matchstick Mini washes his hands after going to the toilet, he loves to wash his hands. Matchstick Mini thinks washing his hands is fun. Matchstick Mini knows which tap is hot and which one is cold, he is very clever.

When Matchstick Mini comes home, he takes his dirty shoes off at the door. Matchstick Mini does not want the floors to get dirty, Matchstick Mini is very clever, and he leaves his shoes at the door.

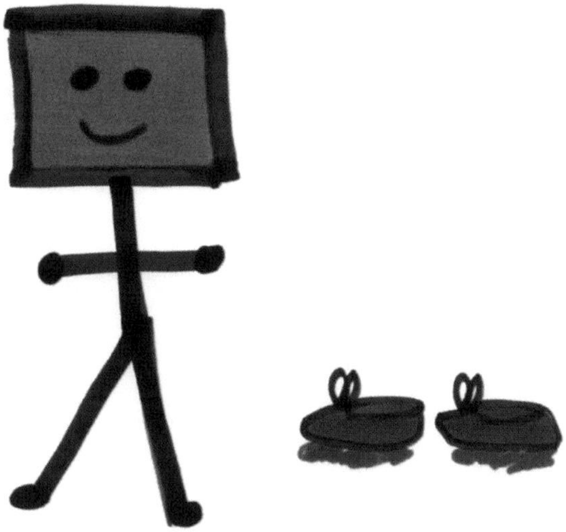

Matchstick Mini always tells people if their shoelace is open, Matchstick Mini is kind and clever, he does not want someone to trip and fall.

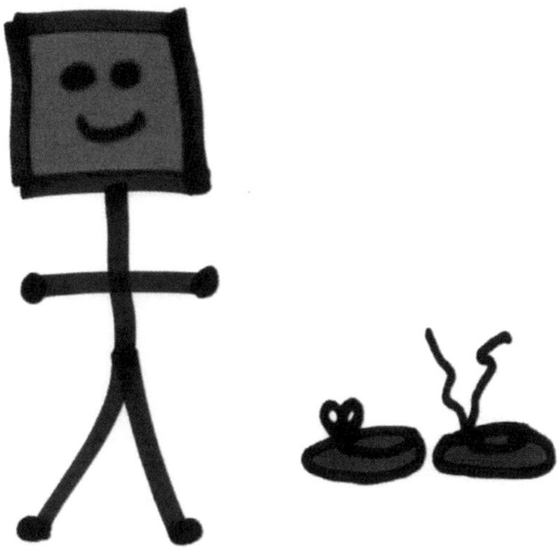

Matchstick Mini always stays near adults when he goes out, he knows that adults would be upset if he got lost. Matchstick Mini always tells someone where he is going, Matchstick Mini is very clever.

Matchstick Mini knows that you should only throw stones into water for fun, Matchstick Mini would never throw stones at other people or other things, he knows that would be very silly.

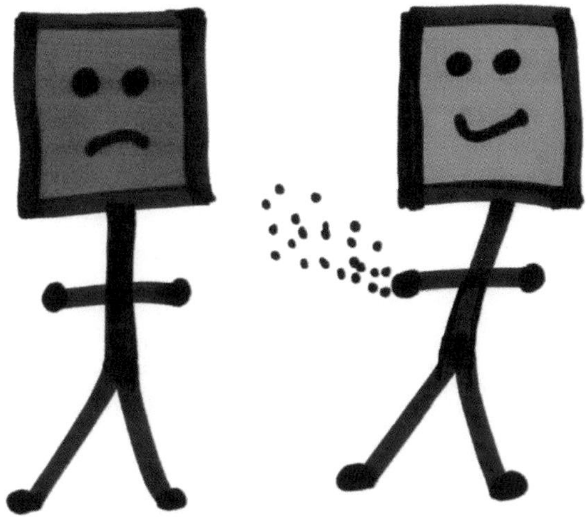

Matchstick Mini is clever, he knows what things he should and shouldn't throw, he throws balls and Frisbees and has lots of fun. Matchstick Mini likes to throw stones into the water when he is at the seaside for fun too.

Matchstick Mini knows that throwing rubbish on the ground is not good. Matchstick Mini is very clever, he puts his rubbish in the bin, he likes to pretend putting rubbish in the bin is a game. Matchstick Mini likes to make things fun. Do you put your rubbish in the bin like Matchstick Mini?

Matchstick Mini wears his seatbelt in the car, he won't put his head or hands out of the car window, he knows that is silly. Matchstick Mini is very clever.

Matchstick Mini knows that he is not allowed to write on the walls and furniture, he writes on paper and loves to draw. Matchstick Mini has a blackboard too and he loves to write on his blackboard with chalk and has lots of fun with this too.

Matchstick Mini knows electricity is dangerous, he knows that electrical sockets and wires are not toys. Matchstick Mini is very clever, he only plays with his toys.

Matchstick Mini won't touch real tools, Matchstick Mini knows they can be dangerous, he likes to play with his toys.

When Matchstick Mini is finished playing with his toys he likes to tidy up, Matchstick Mini does not want his toys to get broken, he likes to look after his toys. Do you look after your toys like Matchstick Mini?

Printed in Great Britain
by Amazon

32718688R00021